us

feeds the
people

illustrated by Gordon Stowell

Wherever He went Jesus was followed by crowds of people. They wanted to hear more from this wonderful teacher. They wanted to hear more about how God loves all of us.

The crowds had followed Jesus one day. They had come out of the villages and towns to hear Him. Many of them had walked for miles. There were men and women, children and old folks, sick people and well people.

All day long Jesus spoke to them.
He healed those who were sick.
He comforted the sad. He made them
all happy.

In the evening everybody was tired and hungry. There was no food for them out in the wilderness.

"You should send them all back
home, Master," his friends said.
"Let them go back to the villages
and buy food for themselves."

Jesus said, "No. Let them stay longer. You give them something to eat."

"How on earth can we feed them?"
wondered the friends. All they could
find were five small loaves and two
fishes. They belonged to a young
boy. "Bring them to me," said Jesus.
The boy handed the food to Jesus.

There were well over five thousand people in the crowd and Jesus' friends were puzzled, "What use will five little loaves and two fishes be among so many?"

Jesus got everyone to sit down on the grass in groups of hundreds and

groups of fifties. When they had settled down He took the loaves and fishes and thanked God for them.

He passed the food to his friends and they gave it out to the hungry people.

Everybody in the whole crowd had enough to eat, and when they cleaned up afterwards there were twelve baskets full of crumbs left.

How pleased the young boy must have been to see how God had fed so many people with his small gift.

Little Fish Books about Jesus

JESUS
is born

Little Fish Books about Jesus

JESUS
heals

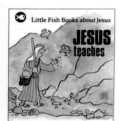

Little Fish Books about Jesus

JESUS
teaches

Little Fish Books about Jesus

JESUS
loves

Little Fish Books